Beneath the Armagh Sky - Growing Up on Spring Farm

By Sandra Davidson

About The Author

Sandra Davidson presently resides in Laurencetown, a delightful village just outside the town of Banbridge in Northern Ireland. The people of Laurencetown are wonderful and so welcoming.

She is a civil servant and has worked in various departments in the NICS.

Sandra decided to write this book as she and her siblings, sisters, Brenda, Lesley, Amanda, Melanie, and Gail, and her brother Derek, always took delight in their upbringing on the family farm close to Armagh City. It gave them hours of fun, exploring every nook and cranny in the big house and the outbuildings.

Enjoy the fun they had!

Dedication

This book is dedicated to the following people who are no longer with us:

My Sister, Brenda Davidson

My Father, Walter Davidson J.P. (Justice of the Peace)

My Paternal Grandparents, William Davidson J.P. (Justice of the Peace)

Margaret Davidson,

My Maternal Grandparents, Joseph Magwood and Margaret (Peggy) Magwood

Forever in our hearts.

Introduction

This is a story of children of primary school age, growing up on a beautiful farm on the outskirts of Armagh City. They were delighted to spend hours playing in the magnificent garden and backyards. Hiding behind the mature trees and bushes, and in the numerous sheds the farm had to offer, was one of their favourite pastimes.

The time they had with their grandparents, and the good grounding in life they received from their parents, all added to the people they have become, and they will always be grateful for the childhood they had, growing up in a privileged lifestyle.

The story also follows the children's lives attending a country primary school with friends, their love for music and trips to Belfast, and the fun times in the numerous rooms of the farmhouse. It was even better when it rained, as that meant the children could still play and not get in the way of the grown-ups too much.

Christmas was an exciting time for everyone, as well as a noisy one, since there were seven children to keep occupied on Christmas Day. The early start to church for the carol service and the children rushing home to get back to playing with the toys from Santa Claus was enough to keep everyone busy.

Summer holidays were necessary for time to play in the sunshine and let the children's imaginations run wild as they thought of different games to play late into the long summer evenings.

Overall, it is a delightful story of happiness, of a loving family, and of how that happiness has carried the children **through** to being adults and to the lives they all now lead.

I hope everyone enjoys the book, and if it is successful, I will write another one on the years from eleven till early twenties, and after that, the years from early twenties to the present day. A trilogy awaits!

- Sandra Davidson

Table of Contents

Chapter 1: Glorious Spring Farm 1

Chapter 2: Summer Holidays 7

Chapter 3: Primary School 18

Chapter 4: Christmas at Spring Farm 30

Chapter 5: Chores 41

Chapter 6: Grandparents 48

Chapter 7: Music 66

Chapter 8: Imaginary Friends 74

Chapter 9: Trips to the Big Smoke 78

Photographs 85

Chapter 1: Glorious Spring Farm

Growing up on Spring Farm was a charming experience. The love from our parents, the beautiful surrounding fields, and the large garden where we played for hours, especially during the long summer evenings, are something we can never forget.

Our home was always full of fun and laughter and was quite noisy most of the time. Spring Farm is located on the edge of the endearing city of Armagh, the ecclesiastical capital of Ireland. Close by, two enchanting cathedrals overlook the shops and houses below. The town is full of history and Georgian buildings; it is also the Georgian capital of Northern Ireland. From the avenue at the farm, you can have a magnificent view of the city. You can also watch the sunrise and sunset over the town from there, and at night, the twinkling of lights in the town make it look magical. Watching the sunset over Armagh from the field at the farm was enchanting and something I enjoy even today.

The farm itself was always remarkably busy. It was home to a herd of cows, sheds full of pigs, calves, and hens. It was busy non-stop the entire year round for Daddy and the farm workers. The house was grand with numerous rooms and halls. There were two front doors and two back doors. In fact, at one point, it used to have three back doors. It was good for us as it meant we had many doors to escape through if we had been naughty and needed to make a quick escape from our parents. Those doors also gave us hours of fun when our friends arrived, and we would spend time running in and out, playing hide-and-seek. Little did we realise, but we probably drove our parents insane with the noise.

The many rooms consisted of a large dining room, three sitting rooms, a kitchen, a scullery, and a larder, which was turned into two kitchens in the early 1970s, two staircases, 6 bedrooms, a bathroom, and an extra drawing room with a beautiful, ornate sofa. You couldn't miss the grand pictures of the Queen and the Duke of Edinburgh as you passed through this room to get to the bathroom. Two of the bedrooms were so big that they could have held two large double beds and a single bed, and there would still be room for more furniture. Before we had our playroom, there was space in those two bedrooms where we would play with our toys, especially on chilly winter days.

There were a front hall and two back halls. One of the back halls led to an old dairy that was in use when my grandfather ran the farm, and that was where he used to fill the milk churns (Spring Farm Dairy) before delivering them around the local area. We have bottles that my grandfather used to hold the milk, and they have Spring Farm Dairy written on them – treasured items! My grandparents had a housekeeper who was still employed by them when my mum married my father and went to live at the farm.

Outside, we had so much room to play in the two backyards, the long avenue, and the large garden at the front of the house, which led to a long driveway. Inside, some of the rooms had magnificent antiques on display that my grandparents had bought over the years. All of them were displayed with pride. A beautiful piano still sits in one of the rooms at the front of the house. As soon as I was able to have piano lessons to learn to play it, there was no stopping me. Every chance I got, I disappeared to the piano room, as we always called it. My father could play the piano quite well, and my sister, Amanda, took piano lessons, too. I often pretended I was playing the organ in church and would pretend to hold a full church service on my own. It took quite a while to get through it!

So, there we were, Brenda, Lesley, Sandra, Amanda, Derek, Melanie, and Gail, living our wonderful, fun-filled lives on our beautiful farm. Of course, we would have the odd little sibling disagreement from time to time, but overall, we were incredibly good together. We all had great imaginations when it came to deciding how to play a new game we came up with, or what prank to play on someone.

One of the warmest memories of living there was the fact that music always filled the house. The record player would be on full blast, playing all the latest hits on the charts. We danced around the rooms, taking care not to knock anything down, and sang along. I am not sure how our parents dealt with the mayhem.

One of our favourite pastimes was sliding down the curved banister at the front stairs, from which we all took a tumble. I am surprised it is still there to this day and in one piece. One thing that did frighten us, especially me, was a walking stick that was kept on the hallstand in the front hall. It had a carved head of a fox, and the mouth was open, showing its teeth. I always hated having to walk past it on a dark night and would look the other way. Of course, it was one of my grandparents' antique walking sticks and could not be moved!

Under the stairs was a cupboard where we placed our toys. It contained: Charlie the toy horse, a toy dog named Judy and numerous prams, dolls, tractors, and bicycles. Later, our parents changed one of the bedrooms into a playroom for us, and we could play and store our toys in it, which meant not making a mess in the front hall for visitors to see!

In the front garden stood two beautiful Victorian greenhouses. They were a considerable size, and a lot of vegetables and fruit were grown in them. We helped our grandmother and our great-aunts pick the fresh lettuce and tomatoes for tea for the farm workers on summer evenings. I loved watering the fruit and vegetables as it usually meant turning the hose towards my siblings and soaking them or anyone that was close by in the greenhouse with me!

Unfortunately, the greenhouses are no longer there as they made way for a larger lawn at the farm – I will have to admit I always missed them as they were part of our life when we were growing up.

Chapter 2: Summer Holidays

Summer was a fun time at the farm. The school holidays arrived, and the sun was shining. It was time to go out and play!

We mostly played in the large garden at the front of the house on the farm. It was, and still is, a place filled with secluded spots, a spacious lawn, well-tended flowerbeds, and a long avenue perfect for riding our bikes or roller skating at breakneck speed.

My siblings and I ventured out early in the morning, all dressed in summer clothes that consisted of colourful shorts, t- shirts and sandals, and then in the afternoon, when it became much warmer, the girls were in swimsuits, and my brother wore his swimming trunks. I did not think we realised how much of a tan we were getting, as we were always too busy sorting out our next adventure.

We used the petals from the gorgeous roses and sweet pea to mark out our houses and cycling lanes. Or if there happened to be a wedding in that day's events, we used the petals of the flowers as confetti. We used Mummy's old dresses to dress up in for the make-believe weddings, and old lace curtains were put to effective use for the wedding dress for whoever we chose to be the bride.

Our pets joined in on the fun. The dogs barked at our laughter and ran after us as we ran about the lawn, covering each other in freshly cut grass. The cattle in the front field stopped whatever they were at and glanced our way to watch, wondering what was happening.

Mummy or my grandmother would call us in for lunch and tea. We gladly went in for a bite to eat, as all the energy we used made us all feel quite hungry.

Lunch always consisted of three courses, no matter what time of the year it was or how many people were there for lunch. Afterwards, we helped with the dishes, which was like a conveyor belt as we stood in a row handing one dish after another to each of us, as one washed the dishes and a couple of us dried them, and then a couple of us put the dishes in the cupboards. After we had completed that chore, we were on our way for another few hours of fun in the sun.

We played tennis in the square tarmacked area in the garden, as Wimbledon was a must for us to watch, and we re-enacted some of the matches, imitating our favourite tennis players. I was always Virginia Wade and put my hair up like the way she wore hers, and I took great delight when she won the Women's Singles Final in 1977. Unfortunately, too many windows were broken, much to the dismay of our parents! Thank goodness they realised it was all part of growing up and never made too much of a fuss if the ball landed in the kitchen after smashing through the windowpane. They always warned us to be more careful the next time, though.

The long summer evenings, and of course, no school, meant that we could stay up a bit later. I was sure my parents were delighted with that, as it meant that when we eventually went to bed, we were so tired we fell asleep, and they had a bit of time to themselves to relax.

I loved walking around in my bare feet in the summer, as it always felt like freedom to me. We had cuts and bruises from falling off our bikes, although this did not deter us from coming down the hill on the front avenue. We raced each other as fast as we could go, and when we got to the bottom of the hill, we turned and went back up again for another race. It was a healthy competition.

Our roller skates were made of metal, were laced at the front, and had a strap that buckled around our legs to keep them in place. We thought we were the bees' knees with them! We started at the top of the lane and raced each other, usually tripping over ourselves, and if we did make it to the bottom of the hill, we glided onto the lawn to stop ourselves. Such fun! It was a miracle we did not end up in the casualty ward with the tumbles we had.

The banks on the lawn gave the garden character, and they are still there today. I remember a big tree that grew on part of the lawn, and Daddy decided to take it down. On being taken down, the tree fell towards the house and covered most of the tarmacked area. It looked bigger than it did when it was standing. With the tree away from that part of the lawn, it gave us more free space to play, especially on the banks! Of course, my siblings and I put them to wonderful use. We rolled ourselves as well as our easter eggs down them. We sometimes tried going down them on our bikes and roller skates, although those efforts usually ended in a bad fall.

We also put the backyard to clever use. We played football games and cricket there, although the games usually took place in the evening, as it was always busy with tractors and cars coming and going during the day. Unfortunately, it meant more windowpanes were smashed due to some of us whacking the cricket ball towards the farmhouse!

The farm itself was a hive of activity during the summer months, and the sound of tractors and machinery in the fields into the wee small hours of the morning was quite a common thing. My father and his workers always tried to get the jobs done in case there was rain forecast.

Everyone ended up with a tan, and the nights were very warm, and the windows in our bedrooms were kept open to help cool us down.

We always enjoyed having no homework for the two months of summer, and it was always a shock for the system when we went back to school in September.

We, of course, were off from school the full two months of July and August and, being from a Protestant family, we celebrated the Twelfth of July. The night before, Daddy got prepared for the following day, and he was in a local band belonging to our church known as Kildarton Accordion Band, which led Kildarton Lodge No. 540. Mummy sorted out our clothes and she dressed us very smartly. The day started early as Daddy had to be away to Kildarton Orange Hall, where the band and the lodge gathered before marching into town from near the end of the avenue at our farm.

There was always a fry prepared for us on the 12th of July morning, and we enjoyed good fried bacon, sausages, fried eggs, potato bread, and fried soda bread – just delicious. It kept us going all day.

We then all got into the car and sat at the end of the avenue to watch Daddy's band pass by and followed them part of the way into Armagh. In town, we parked outside our grandparents' house on the Mall and were able to watch all the other bands and Orange Lodges gather at the local Orange Hall before they set off to march around the town. It was fun, and we waved little flags, and you could hear people calling out to the people they knew who were marching. It was like a carnival atmosphere. After the march through the centre of the town, the bands and the lodges then got on buses and headed off to the Field where the main demonstration was being held that year. In the county of Armagh, it rotates around the different towns every eleven years.

The main Twelfth of July celebration was also held, and still is to this day, in one of our fields close to the farm when it was Armagh's turn to host the main demonstration. From early morning to the late hours on the eleventh night, and in fact sometimes during the week before, people were in the field putting up tents and displays. For us, it was great excitement watching it all take place so close to us.

A week at Cranfield Caravan Park was always a special time for us as a family. My Granny and Granda Magwood always booked a caravan beside the one we had booked, or one close by.

The summers were usually quite hot then, and of course, we spent time on the beach, building sandcastles and scrambling in and out of the water. We looked for jellyfish on the beach and screamed when we located them. Picking beautiful shells and stones always ended up with us bringing a load of them back home.

My grandparents always had a puzzle to build during their stay at Cranfield, and any time we were in their caravan, we tried to help. This activity lasted the full week of our stay and was incredibly engaging for everyone. We always tried to get it finished before the end of our holiday.

Friends and relatives would call with us for a visit at the caravan, and it was an exciting time for catching up. We travelled to Kilkeel, the nearest town to the caravan park, during the week and visited the shops. Mrs Newell's was our favourite, as it was a toy shop, and Mummy let us get something out of it. It was always a treat, and I remember playing with the toys I got for hours at the caravan.

It was always lovely waking up each morning and peeking out the window of the caravan to see the lighthouse and glorious blue water. At night, when the lights were out, you could watch the light from the lighthouse going round and listen to the foghorn when a dense fog descended in the area. From time to time, a cargo ship passed up Carlingford Lough and would excite us tremendously as seeing something so grand far out in the water. The binoculars were out, and my sister Brenda loved reading the writing on the side and always let us know the name of the ship. We took photos of the ships, and in later years, when videos came along, part of the holiday videos included a ship passing Cranfield in the water near the lighthouse – the Bolero Contessa being one of them.

We made friends at Cranfield and played with them in the sandpits that were scattered around the caravan site. Nowadays, the sandpits have disappeared, as they would be seen as a health and safety issue and just as well, as people would trip and fall into them, especially at night. We gave some characters we met on holiday at the caravan park nicknames. One such person we named Scallion, in other words, 'Spring Onion' – I really did not know why, but the name suited him.

I loved going to the Lighthouse Café. It had a jukebox and the teenagers had it playing all the hits on the charts at the time. One song that the holiday makers seem to love is Summer Holiday by Cliff Richard! It was quite apt for a holiday park.

When it came time to go home, we were quite sad, as it would be another year before we would visit again. We always asked Daddy to buy a caravan, and we nearly succeeded once and thought we had convinced him it would be a promising idea. Unfortunately, our requests never happened, as he said that he would have been afraid of us travelling on the roads to the caravan park, as parts of them were twisty and dangerous.

The older pupils always looked after the younger ones, and there were always the favourite children that everyone wanted to be friends with.

A part of the day that children in P1 to P3 at the primary school liked was when Mrs Armstrong put the radio on and we listened and danced to the programme 'Music and Movement'. We listened to the voice on the radio telling us to stretch and jump to the music playing, and we did it with laughter and playfulness. The programme was from the School Broadcasting Council for the United Kingdom, which had been set up in 1947 and had come to play a part in the education of children at that time. I loved the dancing and having my little gym shoes on. We had to wear those shoes so as not to mark the floor. We danced around the chairs and desks, laughing and giggling as we went along.

In the afternoon, the youngest children all brought their tiny chairs to the front of the classroom and listened intently to the stories on 'Listen with Mother.' The show always started with the phrase, "Are you sitting comfortably? Then I'll begin." The phrase became so well known that it appeared in The Oxford Dictionary of Quotations and has also been incorporated and sampled by many artists and musicians, one being Doctor Who! The radio show always indicated to the children that they were close to the end of the school day and would all soon be collected by their parents to take them home. All our little faces looked towards the door to see if we could see whose parents had arrived through the little windowpanes.

We did not have to wear a school uniform at Wastelands Primary School, and therefore we had the choice, or should I say our parents had the choice, as to what we wore. My grandmother was a great knitter, and Mummy dressed us in the cardigans or jumpers that my grandmother would knit for us. I remember the lovely royal blue cardigans she knit for us, and we are seen wearing them in some photographs of us at the school. It was good too that the girls could wear trousers in winter, whereas in other primary schools where a uniform was compulsory, the girls still had to wear their skirts during the cold months. Although nowadays it has all changed, and girls can now wear trousers in winter. A good change to be honest.

When the time came to move into the headmaster's classroom, it was quite daunting for pupils, as suddenly everything seemed that bit harder. We had to study fractions, and the bigger words were more difficult to spell. We spent the afternoons studying instead of listening to the radio and having a more relaxing time in Mrs Armstrong's classroom.

PE was, however, like a workout for the army. Our principal had been in the army and had fought in the war, and he must have thought we were his soldiers. We had to get into line and march around the playground, and if you were out of step, you got a furious telling-off! We skipped and threw balls to each other for our aim and reflex actions. We all laughed and enjoyed it, but the principal kept quite a close eye on us and made sure we were performing the exercises and not slacking. I must admit we still talk about our PE lessons at primary school.

There was also the Penguin book club, where we were able to buy books and the teachers ordered them for us. I was a great fan of the Laura Ingalls Wilder books and bought the full set of the Little House on the Prairie books. Friday afternoon was set aside for the headmaster to read to us, and the pupils just loved it when he read from those books, as Laura and her family had so many adventures, and the books told the story of a young girl's life from when she was a small child until she got married. I had always loved reading, and those books were my entertainment at home too.

Going home was quite something. The teacher, Mrs Armstrong, would have given us a lift – myself, my siblings, and other pupils. There were so many of us that the car was stuffed and, in those days, nobody wore seatbelts and so we were all sitting on top of each other. There were times when school was finished, but the teacher was not ready to go, and so we started to walk home, and we would try to get as far down the road before the teacher came along to bring us the rest of the way. Being astute children, we knew to keep close to the side when cars came along and always looked out for each other. We chatted as we went along and picked berries from the hedges or little primroses growing on the banks.

Some afternoons, my sister, Amanda, and I had piano lessons at Mrs Hayes' house, and it meant not getting home until a bit later. Not only did we have school lessons, Amanda and I had music lessons to practise on the piano too. Believe me, it was a long day when that happened!

The piano was and still is in a living room at the front of the house, and it is so beautiful. It has an expensive design and would have cost my grandparents a lot of money when they purchased it. I am not sure where my grandparents bought it, but it was one of their best purchases ever.

We also used the piano room to hold our birthday parties. Mummy would put a large cover over the big round table and place the chairs for us to sit on around it. I am sure Mummy was always glad when the parties finished, as there were so many pieces of antique furniture and ornaments in that room that could have been destroyed by all our playfulness.

There are fabulous photographs of us at Wastelands Primary School. One includes my sisters, Lesley and Brenda, my cousin, Colin Ewart, who now lives near Victoria, Vancouver Island, BC, Canada and with whom we catch up by FaceTime, and me. Colin only attended Wastelands for a few years before transferring to the Armstrong Primary School in Armagh. Another photograph is of Brenda and Lesley looking like two professors with their beautiful little round glasses – the glasses would now be classified as fashionable. In those days, you were thought to be a nerd for wearing any type of glasses. How times have changed.

I must admit the clothes we wore in many of those photos back then are now back in fashion, and so it is true that style does turn full circle! Brilliant!

Mummy would leave us at school every morning, and we would call for a lovely family, the Nesbitts, at the Lough Lane on the Hamiltonsbawn Road and take them with us. As I have mentioned, we never wore seatbelts, as they were not compulsory for a decade later, and we were all packed in like sardines in the front and back of the car. The Nesbitt family then moved house; in fact, they moved closer to our farm and have been our family's fantastic friends and neighbours for decades. Always so kind and helpful.

On one occasion, I was left behind at school and still to this day, I do not know how it happened. I had gone to use the lavatory, and when I came out, the teacher had left with the other children in the car. I could not believe it and, of course, being so young and so small, I started to cry and panic. The headmaster was still there, so I knew I would still get home, but decided to walk to my aunt and uncle's farmhouse near the school. My Aunt Sarah opened the door and could see I was in a state of distress. She got me settled and then phoned Mummy to tell her where I was. I sat and did my spellings until Mummy came over to pick me up. I have never really got over that time and the shock and panic of being left behind at school. It still haunts me to this day.

In winter, we all gathered round the radiator and watched the rain and snow fall on the playground. We played games in the cloakrooms, and these games consisted of hiding between the coats hanging from the hooks or beside the cupboards in the corridor. The school was quite small, so we only had a handful of games we could play.

Suddenly, or so it seemed, it was time to leave Wastelands Primary School and move on in the world to adulthood, to a different school, and get ready for life in the years ahead!

Chapter 4: Christmas at Spring Farm

Christmas at Spring Farm was always a joyous occasion. We would get up early for church, half asleep as we had been up in the small hours checking to see what toy Santa Claus had brought. Our parents must have been delighted with us waking them up so early, excitedly showing them the toys and stocking fillers from Santa.

The church service was held in the beautiful, quaint church of Kildarton on the Hamiltonsbawn Road out of Armagh. On Christmas morning, everyone, including the minister, was itching to get home and get the dinner on and have time with their family before all the festivities would commence.

We filled our family pew in the church, as there were so many of us, and Daddy would take his place in the choir.

The service was full of Christmas cheer, and the readings were about the birth of Jesus. The congregation was in full voice singing carols, and when the service finished, the minister would shake our hands on the way out and wish everyone a merry Christmas. There was chatter after the service as the children were showing toys to other members of the congregation. The service did not last as long as it usually did on a Sunday, as this was a special day for families and everyone wanted to get home quickly.

When we arrived home from church, Mummy would put the kettle on for tea, and we would put the TV on and watch Christmas programmes. Our favourite was the hour-long comedy show, Laurel and Hardy, Buster Keaton, and the Keystone Cops! Such fun!

We would switch the lights on the Christmas trees, of which there were three at Spring Farm, before we would have gone to church. We had one tree in the small family room that was used as an overflow room for the day until bedtime, because so many people came to the farm on Christmas Day, and the larger room would fill up very quickly, and we needed an extra room to sit in. One tree in the larger sitting room and one exceptionally large Christmas tree in the hallway beside the spiral staircase. The tree in the hallway was a remarkable sight, as it was so tall and decorated with colourful tinsel, old-fashioned Christmas baubles, and numerous Christmas tree lights.

Even though everyone would be looking forward to the delicious dinner, we would have played with our toys for a period beforehand. The chatter between us all would have been to check and see what Santa had eaten from the food we had left for him, and if one of us had heard him and his reindeer at the house.

I remember my first doll, I called her Nicola, and I still have her to this day. She was a sixties doll and wore a black and white striped coat, red dress, and long red boots. Nicola always reminds me of Nancy Sinatra singing the song "These Boots are made for Walkin'." All the dolls I received from Santa, I have kept, and some are still in their boxes. I still love my dolls, Kate, Sheena, Sindy, Nicola, Tracy, Jennifer, and little Rose.

One thing that most children looked forward to receiving back then for a present was a Christmas Annual — whether it was Jackie, Beano, or one of the other firm favourites. These proved to be a great talking point when we returned to school after the Christmas holidays.

Most of us sat around the large table in the main kitchen for Christmas dinner, although sometimes we had to use an extra table to help with the overflow of people. The noise would spill over into the kitchen. Dinner was served around 1 pm. It started with homemade vegetable soup, followed by the turkey dinner, and then dessert. By that stage, we were all full and could not eat another thing. Unfortunately for us, we then had to wash the dishes! Of course, there were leftovers, which were used for dinner on Boxing Day, and possibly for dinners later in the week. We never got tired of eating turkey.

Daddy had turkeys for Christmas at the farm, and when the time came to sell them, the phone never stopped ringing as the demand for his turkeys was always something to behold.

I found the conversation around the Christmas dinner table fascinating. The adults would be recalling events that had happened during the year, ones that we had never heard of, and we would be listening as they spoke. Children talked amongst themselves and tried to guess what the presents under the Christmas tree would be and who they would be from.

For the evening meal on Christmas Day, there would be a buffet assembled on the kitchen table, as we were all feeling quite peckish by then.

Mummy's cooking was always so tasty, and I enjoyed the preparation on Christmas Eve — my speciality being making the breadcrumbs for the stuffing. I devoured the crusts as people would have said they gave you brains!

Mummy cleaned the house from top to bottom. In fact, she would have the decorators before Christmas, preparing the house for all the visitors. She could have been seen on her knees polishing the red cardinal tiles on the kitchen floor and back hall late into the evening on Christmas Eve. I am sure she was exhausted.

We always wondered if there would be snow on Christmas morning. If there was, we would have a snowball fight or get our sleighs out or better still, roll about in the snow. This was, of course, to the dismay of our parents as they were preparing for a busy day ahead.

If the snow lasted for a few days, we would be out in it playing, even taking a plastic bag to the hills in our fields, and we would sit on it and slide down the hill at speed, squealing and laughing.

The fields, covered in snow, around the farm were beautiful to look at, especially at night when you could see the snow glistening in the distance.

Friends and relatives would sometimes arrive in the afternoon on Christmas Day, and cups of tea were made, and there was more chatter. We played board games and had quizzes – all the usual Christmas entertainment.

At 3 pm, the Queen would be on the television with her yearly address to the nation. If we were being too boisterous, our grandmother would tell us to hush, as she always looked forward to this part of the day religiously every year!

After, one of us would give out the presents from under the tree, and we would open them with great enjoyment. We would throw the Christmas wrapping paper from every corner of the room — in fact, our parents told us we had more fun with the paper instead of enjoying the presents we had received.

We devoured more food later in the evening, in the form of turkey sandwiches, mini sausage rolls, cocktail sausages on sticks, creamy chicken vol-au-vents, and Christmas cake or pudding. You would have thought we had never seen food, especially after the vast amount of food we had consumed at lunchtime. However, we could not wait to fill our bellies again and would be reaching across the table to grab our favourites. I always had a soft spot for the *vol-au-vents* and the small sausage rolls. Nowadays, there is more on offer for buffet foods, spicy chicken pieces, mini pizzas, chicken drumsticks, small quiches, and loads more, but the golden oldies are still available. It would not be the same without them.

A lot of discussion took place at the table at the evening buffet. The chatter was about the day's excitement and all that had happened. Right from when we woke up and found our toys from Santa to the church service, the Christmas lunch, and the opening of the presents. The girls got new dolls, and we would compare and discuss names for them. We would be pulling crackers and checking out whatever we found inside them, and we would all put the obligatory cracker hats on and have a laugh at them. If anybody put their hat on crooked, we would call them stupid!

We were always so tired by the evening and usually glad to get to bed, even with all the excitement of Christmas Day.

Boxing Day was just as joyful as we had more time with our toys we had received from Santa.

The dinner was the same as the previous day, although there was more room at the table and not as many dishes to wash and put away.

There would be more visits from relatives along with more chatter about how they had spent Christmas and what they had received as presents. Tea and snacks would be served along with sandwiches and festive biscuits. We did not have coffee as a beverage at that time, but we had plenty of hot tea. Now it seems as though coffee has overtaken tea in the stakes for best hot drink. I cannot seem to get through a day now without having a latte.

I always enjoyed the Christmas films, my favourite being Mary Poppins, and still is to this day. White Christmas was also a firm favourite, and we would have sung along with our parents to all the songs from it. It starred Bing Crosby, Danny Kaye, Vera

Ellen, and Rosemary Clooney. (Gorgeous George's aunt!)

Next on the agenda was New Year's Eve, and again there was a flurry of excitement in preparation as visitors called at the farm to wish us a happy New Year. Party poppers were set off, and we all waited anxiously in case we missed the strike of Big Ben to welcome in the new year. Food was prepared for the evening ahead, and everyone gathered around the table to eat the delights. When midnight struck, we all joined hands and sang Auld Lang Syne - there were also some tears for people who were no longer with us. Then it was off to bed and the sense of a fresh start to a new year.

Of course, throughout the Christmas and New Year celebrations, the farm work had to continue, and Daddy would have to attend to the animals while we partied inside. The work on a farm is unending, and demanding work is the order of the day. Dear help Daddy, he could hear all the laughter and talking in the house while he was doing the chores in the farmyard.

In the days following, to our dismay, we would have to take down the Christmas decorations, and the house would seem quite empty and bare for a while until we got back to the usual humdrum of our daily lives. School would be starting soon, and following a few months, Easter would arrive, and we would be off on more school holidays. Yippee!

Chapter 5: Chores

Yes, it is true, we all had something to do at Spring Farm — whether it was helping to clean out the pig houses, gathering eggs, or washing the floors after tea — all the same, it was good fun and helped instil a great work ethic in all of us, and it is something that has lasted to this day.

I always loved the summer holidays when my grandfather was alive, and I would get up early and help him feed and tend the little calves. The calves were so cute, and they would flick their tails when they saw us arriving with the milk and the meal. Their coats were usually all different colours, most commonly black and white, although I loved them all. The calves adored getting their noses stroked, and I obliged every time. I cannot remember helping him in the evenings, as I was preoccupied playing in the orchard or with my dolls.

There were always quite a few workers at the farm at various times of the year, and of course, they had to be fed. Mummy never left the kitchen during those times, checking on the dinner of which there were usually three courses. It was like a hotel. Soup for starters, a main course of mince, or some sort of meat, and potatoes. A dessert of tart and custard or some other delight, and then of course a cup of tea. This meant there would be dishes galore to be washed and dried and put away in the cupboards. I never enjoyed washing the pots and pans as the food was sometimes hard to remove, and we sorted the leftovers to reuse — no waste in those days. The dogs were well fed if it was not possible to reheat the leftover food.

On Saturdays, we cleaned the house from top to bottom. First, we changed the sheets on the beds and put new ones on. One of us would clean the front part of the house, where the front rooms were, and one of us would clean the bathroom, and down the back stairs. It took a few hours as some of the rooms were so big that it took time to hoover them. I do not think any of us were ever enamoured with having to do housework at the weekend! We were always careful when we were dusting under any of the antiques that belonged to my grandparents, as they would have been expensive and of sentimental value. From time to time, the cupboards got a good spring clean, and it took longer to get the housework finished as there were ornaments everywhere.

I spent some of my summer holidays washing the clothes with Mummy's new twin-tub washing machine. I thought it was great putting clothes in one side for washing and then the other for rinse and spin. It did keep me out of mischief for hours, as coming from a big family, there were so many clothes to wash every day of every week. I am sure I must have destroyed some of them as I probably put them in a temperature with whites from time to time. Ah, well, not to worry, as we could wear those clothes about the farm.

The area used to wash the clothes (nowadays known in every household as the utility room) is still known as the old dairy, as it is where my grandfather would have filled up the milk churns before he delivered the milk around the country.

Of course, we would get tired of our chores and would huff and puff about them. Especially when we knew our friends would be out walking around the town having a fun time. Nevertheless, we would behave and get to work on the chores that our parents assigned to us. It is funny when you are young, and one minute you are huffing and the next you are laughing and enjoying yourself in a matter of minutes, as good parents know what to say to pacify children. It happened all the time.

Our parents would have made our chores fun to do, too. When we cleaned the eggs, we would sing and try to beat each other and check to see who had cleaned the most eggs. We used small scrubbers covered in a small strip of soft sandpaper. In the years that followed, Daddy bought an egg cleaner. It looked like a wheel, covered in what seemed like a soft sponge, and when the egg was held against it as the wheel was turning, it cleaned the egg. I broke quite a few eggs using that machine as I found it difficult to get the pressure right — I made a right mess! It took quite a while to clean all the eggs, as we had so many hens. We placed the clean ones in a square egg filler that held about two dozen eggs, and when filled, we placed the fillers in a large egg box, which we also used to play with, and when it was full, we covered them with a lid. Lorries would arrive during the week to collect the egg boxes.

Cleaning out the pig and calf houses was something else. The smell was unbelievable, and even if we were wearing Wellington boots, our clothes smelt of muck and dirt, and we needed a good scrub afterwards. Naturally, we thought all this was great fun and joked when one of us was covered from head to toe in manure.

When Daddy moved the animals from one field to another, we had to stand in gaps along the way to prevent the animals from entering the sheds and continue their way to the proper destination. Springtime was great as the animals that were in the sheds during the winter months were now in the fields, and they loved it. Running and kicking up their heels, rejoicing in their newfound freedom again. We would stand and watch them and would clap our hands and cheer.

Again, as I mentioned earlier, when summer arrived, the farm got a clean-up. The paint brushes would come out, and we helped put the whitewash on the walls. You needed a steady hand to paint the black edging along the bottom of the walls, so we never did that. Our faces, hands, clothes, and hair were covered in white specks of paint, and we had splashed the cement yard too. Thank goodness Mummy was able to remove the paint with hot water and soap.

When the hay was cut and put into bales, it was fun trying to build the haystacks, as we were so small. Our little legs were covered in small scrapes from the pieces of cut hay. We also got to ride on the trailers piled high with bales. Something that would not be allowed today and should not have been allowed then, but we pleaded to get a ride, and we would squeal with delight at being so high up.

The playroom was always left in a mess, and we were always being told to tidy it. Dolls here and there, Lego pieces scattered over the floor, and possibly some of the walls had scribbles on them. I received a fantastic blackboard for a present one Christmas, and I had all assorted colours of chalk to write with, and of course. the dust from the chalk could sometimes end up on the floor, and we would have it on the soles of our shoes and walk it throughout the house. More cleaning to do!!

Overall, yes, we had chores to do, but the work ethic from it all has stood us all in good stead and has lasted a lifetime.

Chapter 6: Grandparents

We adored our grandparents, and they loved all their grandchildren. My grandfather, William Davidson JP, was a respected gentleman in the Armagh area. He had worked hard to build up the farm. It was said on his wedding day that after the ceremony, he was out ploughing the fields. He worked long hours and was up with the larks to complete his chores. He had a great dairy herd and sold and delivered milk around the surrounding areas. I read in a book not long ago that he even delivered the milk during the war. I believe also that after the war was over, local people made an effigy of Hitler, and they wheeled it around the front field at our farm with people from the town and the surrounding area following it and cheering.

He was an avid watcher of the news, and I remember he would take his seat in the small living room, having stoked the fire, and he would listen intently to the BBC 1, 9 o'clock news. Panorama was another of his favourite programmes, along with University Challenge. He listened carefully to what was happening in the world and would give his views aloud sometimes — it was quite funny and interesting to hear what he had to say. An incredibly wise man.

Bedtime was always around 10 pm, even on the weekends, as he was so devoted to the farm and was always up early to complete his chores.

At breakfast, he always had porridge and a cup of tea, and at 10 o'clock, he would come back into the house for a cup of Bovril — I remember he used to give us a spoonful, but none of us liked it. A good old-fashioned drink, full of goodness, is still available in the shops.

Years later my grandfather would spend days in his vegetable garden with his friend, Johnny Harker. A Catholic man and lifelong friend of our family. They would talk about everything that was going on in the world and, of course, how the vegetables were coming along. Long rows of potatoes, lettuce, cabbages, cauliflowers, and peas would flourish due to their gardening skills, and Mummy would use them to add to the freshly prepared meals. Johnny would also get a share to take home with him.

Of course, my grandfather's vegetable garden would be a play area for us as well, as we went around hiding behind the tall plants and jumping over the freshly dug drills to try and escape if we were caught making a mess. My siblings and I would also sample some of the delights, such as the peas and beans straight from the pod, biting and seeing what was inside. I am sure my granda wondered where some of his beloved vegetables had disappeared to!

He was forever tidy and clean, and he cleaned out the sheds most days. A fantastic work ethic that he instilled in us from day one.

Every Saturday evening, he would go into Loudans for a drink with my uncles and would be home by 10 pm, and had supper before heading to bed, as he would not have wanted to miss attending church the next morning. He was an ardent churchgoer and took a great interest in everything to do with Kildarton church.

I remember that if my grandfather went anywhere, he would always wear a suit and a hat. He was a smartly dressed man.

He was an Orangeman in Cloghan LOL, and I can only ever remember him in a car with other elderly Orangemen on the Twelfth of July. The car would have been in the parade following the Orangemen marching for the lodge. Since Cloghan Lodge belonged to Richhill District, he would only have been seen in Armagh on the 12th of July, when the main Twelfth of July parade was held in the city, and the demonstration field would be one of his own fields. It was usually held on the field closest to the town, but in 1975, the Government bought it and built Drumadd Army Barracks on it. We used to sit and watch all the building work going on. Lorries would bring the building materials and then carry away soil, ready for the fieldwork to commence. It was a scorching summer, and we all got a tan from the spot on the field where we were watching all the activity. The Armagh Twelfth of July demonstration still takes place in one of our fields, but it is now closer to the farm.

Granda Davidson was very well respected in the Armagh City and District, as people always said his yes was yes and his no was no! I will always be so proud to be his granddaughter. I wonder if he ever knew that my siblings and I would look in his wardrobe to check if he had his Fox's mints in the little tin - even if he did, he never said.

He loved to hear of his grandchildren doing well, and when I passed my first piano exam, he came into the kitchen to congratulate me, and he was quite tearful. I was young at the time, 7 or 8, but I can remember him being delighted at what I had achieved.

I can still remember the Christmas when he became quite ill and had to go into the hospital. As a child, we did not realise how ill he really was until the call came through on 28th December 1974 that he had passed away. The Christmas decorations had to be taken down, and Mummy put a sheet over the mirror on the dressing table in my grandfather's bedroom. I think it must have been some sort of custom. People then started arriving as soon as the news got out. So many people came to the house for his wake, and they did not stop coming to pay their respects until the day of his funeral.

When they brought my grandfather's remains to the farm, I did not go into the room to see him as I was too frightened, but my siblings did. A couple of my sisters and I went to stay with my maternal grandparents in Armagh, as it was easier for my parents to cope with the crowds that came to the wake.

The day of the funeral was sad, and my first experience of absolute heartache. The funeral was attended by hundreds of people, mostly men, as Protestant women in those days stayed at home and started to prepare the meal for afterwards. A strange feeling entered the house after everyone had left for the church. It was the end of an era. We all watched from the windows as the cortege made its way along the main road, and my aunts were heard crying in the rooms as they knew their father would not be returning to the farm.

My grandfather, to this day, is dearly missed and fondly remembered by all of us — he made us so proud of Spring Farm. He was also known to us as Na Na Beard — courtesy of my sister Lesley. She gave him this pet name when she was little, even though it was a moustache he had!

My paternal grandmother, Margaret Davidson (née Tweedie), was such a jolly person. Rosy cheeked and twinkling eyes. We only knew her for a fleeting time, as we were all young when she passed away. My brother, Derek, was only one year old when she died, and my sisters, Melanie and Gail, never knew her as they were not born until after her death.

Granny Davidson loved looking after us when Mummy went to help on the farm. When my brother was still a baby, at one stage, he was quite ill, and Granny would have sat with him in the bedroom to give Mummy a break.

She wore long dresses and skirts, and of course, the obligatory apron that women seemed to wear in those days from dawn to dusk to protect their clothes. I remember one apron, which was dark green with a red trim, and Mummy wore it years later. There are photos of Mummy wearing the special apron when she was busy during the day and working in the garden.

There are photos showing Granny Davidson in her finery at weddings and gatherings. She was a refined lady and was so fashionable, even for being a farmer's wife! She had the farmhouse looking grand as the rooms had beautiful furniture, and the curtains were made from the best material. They lasted for years. The antique ornaments are still in their places, especially her collection of antique cups and saucers in the glass cabinet in the dining room.

My sister, Lesley, also gave our grandmother a pet name when she was a little girl. Lesley noticed Granny had sore knees, so she called her "Na Na Knee." Yes, we still talk about our grandparents' pet names with uncontrollable laughter at the thought of them.

Granny Davidson died on 24th March 1969. We love looking at the photos of her, especially the one of her on her wedding day. A great memory of a special time.

Our maternal grandparents lived on the Mall in Armagh, and it is where my mummy and her brother, Wendell, grew up. They had a lovely, comfortable, and tidy house, and it was in a delightful location beside the glorious Mall and all its history and close to the town for shopping.

My maternal grandfather, Joseph Magwood, was a very down-to-earth, practical, and witty man. He worked at Tullygoonigan, and he would travel to work on his motorbike. At the weekends, during the summer, he would sit on the Mall wall and watch the cricket. There were times the cricket ball bounced into my grandparents' windowpanes. One ball even went up their front hall. He also watched sports on TV, especially football and rugby. There was always a great interest when the Ireland rugby team played, as Mike Gibson was a relation of my maternal grandmother. I remember Mike's parents, Cameron and Josie, being at my Great-Granny Ewart's funeral.

Granda Magwood was also quite a fastidious person, and everything had to be done properly. He kept everything, no matter how old, in perfect condition. Even jigsaw puzzles lasted years, and not one piece ever went missing.

I remember him brushing his wavy hair, standing in front of the mirror in the living room, for what seemed like an eternity. He always polished his shoes and put them away after wearing them for the day. He never put his shoes or boots in the shoe cupboard with a mark on them.

He enjoyed visiting the farm as there was usually something to occupy him there, whether it was fixing a broken window or putting up a small piece of spouting that had fallen away from the wall. He would have had a great chat with Granny and Granda

Davidson when he was there—this usually would have taken place in the large sitting room that was a firm favourite for a chat, as it was cosy and warm.

There are photographs of our four grandparents at gatherings at the farm or in the living room in the house on the Mall. They always had a lot of fun, and all seemed to get on so well and were able to confide in each other.

Granda Magwood would also have assisted with the housework and kept the backyard spotless. I am sure he loved it when we would be playing out in the yard, and we would hang curtains up on the washing line to divide our little houses off. There was a door which led from the yard to the back of a garage that was beside our grandparents' house. On opening the door, it led to an adventure for us, as we were not meant to be there. A bit like the children in the classic, *The Lion, the Witch, and the Wardrobe*. We would be giggling and running up and down the larger area behind the petrol station. It would only have been for a brief period, as my grandparents were afraid of anyone on the Mall hearing us and informing the owners of the garage.

Relatives would have visited my grandparents, and we would have to sit quietly until they left. My siblings and I would listen to all that the adults were talking about, although for us it seemed to go on too long, as we were itching to get playing again, especially with the suitcase of dolls that was kept under the sofa.

My sister, Brenda, lived with Granda and Granny Magwood when she was growing up, and we would have played for hours with her when we stayed over at weekends. She was such fun and would get up to mischief of all sorts. She had her own little bedroom, and it was very pretty. Her toys lasted forever as Granny and Granda Magwood made sure they were put back in their place at the end of the day.

On Saturday afternoons, we would watch wrestling on the television and my granda could be heard shouting at the various contestants in the ring. Mick McManus was one, and there was always booing from the people in the audience as he was not well-liked, and if any of us were staying over at the time, we would join in and laugh at the whole spectacle.

Granda Magwood was a sporty person himself and played football for Milford along with my great-uncle, Billy Hill.

It was only lately that we found out, to our surprise, that Granda had an uncle, Joseph Cole, who had died on the first day of the Battle of the Somme, 1st July 1916. We could not believe what we were hearing, as no one had ever mentioned this to us when we were growing up, and now suddenly, we realised we had a great-great- uncle who had died during World War I. (Private Joseph Cole, 18467, Royal Irish Fusiliers). His name is engraved on the Thiepval Memorial that is dedicated to the missing soldiers of the war, and he is listed on a memorial to the dead in the grounds of Saint Salvator's Church, situated on the Castle Leslie Estate in Glaslough, in Co Monaghan.

My Granda Magwood died on 15th August 2006 due to a stroke. He had been in hospital for two weeks but been unconscious throughout. We hope he heard us telling him how much we cared for him.

My Granny Magwood was unbelievably funny. She was mischievous, witty, and full of life. It was hard to keep up with her as she was so full of energy — we all say my sister, Lesley, takes after. Granny Magwood, as she never quits cleaning, is always on the go and has so much energy.

Granny was born Margaret Walker Ewart in a beautiful house on the Mall in Armagh — it has since been knocked down, and the supermarket chain Sainsbury's has been built on the site. Her mother, Elizabeth Ewart (born Elizabeth Walker), was born in Scotland — so we have Scottish blood running through our veins. It has been said that Great-Granny Ewart was related to the Rev George Walker, who was the joint Governor of Londonderry during the Siege in 1689. He was killed at the Battle of the Boyne in 1690 and is the subject of the Duke of Schomberg. She grew up in a family of six, so you see, she also had many siblings. They were a very tall family, apart from my granny, who was the smallest. I am sure it felt strange being small in a house where your parents, brothers, and sister were towering over you. She had two brothers who joined the police — they had the height for it — two brothers who lived locally and had great careers, and a sister who, when she married, went to live in Warrenpoint in County Down.

When she was a young woman, my granny had such long hair she was able to sit on it. We have a photo of her with her long hair, and it is so beautiful and shiny, and yes, she could have sat on it. I really do not know how she got it washed and dried.

Granny was an immense help to my mummy when we were growing up, as there were so many of us. Mummy would collect her and bring her to the farm, where she would help prepare lunch for the men from the farm while Mummy dealt with us. She would never stop until dinner was over, and the dishes washed and put away before she got her own lunch. Later in the afternoon,

Mummy would leave Granny back home as she needed to prepare Granda's dinner.

Knitting was a great passion of Granny Magwood's, and as soon as she sat down to watch TV at night, out would come her knitting needles, and she would light up her Gallaghers cigarette and off she would go for hours. She would knit cardigans, scarves, jumpers, and whatever else Mummy wanted for us or if she received a request for a knitted item from a friend or neighbour. Between knitting and crocheting, Granny never got bored.

Two of her favourite programmes were Crossroads, the main character being Meg Richardson as the owner of a motel, and of course Coronation Street, with the cast full of legendary characters such as Ena Sharples, who wore her trademark hair net. On Saturdays, she watched the Generation Game, which starred Bruce Forsyth, and it was good family entertainment.

She was a very tidy lady and never stopped cleaning and dusting her house. From time to time, if I was staying overnight, I loved to clean items on her mantelpiece with Brasso, and it was always worth it as the brass ornaments ended up so shiny. My hands were always black with the Brasso, and it took a while to get them washed properly.

On Saturdays, Granny would be over at Armagh Ruby Club when it was located on the Mall, and she would prepare the meal for the rugby players after the match. We loved going over with her, as we got a chance to run up and down the main hall for a while and then help with setting the tables. We could watch the rugby match from the kitchen windows of the clubhouse. It was noisy when all the players eventually came in for their meal, and then it was clearing up time after they had left.

Holidays at Cranfield with Granny Magwood were the best. She would sit and knit and look out the caravan window, passing remarks about people. Her great wit would come into play when she was describing them. We would be bent over laughing. Walking on the beach from Cranfield to Greencastle was an adventure.

Granny would be dancing and doing a jig to keep us entertained. We roared with laughter when she described the fuchsia growing in the hedge on our walks along the road towards Kilkeel. It was the way she pronounced the word fuchsia, and we knew she was just being mischievous as usual.

My Granda would also comment on the fisherman driving through the caravan park, as he would be sounding his annoying horn to let everyone know he was about and to buy his fresh fish. It was a special moment, and it added to the excitement of being on holiday by the sea.

Granny always dressed so well. I never once saw her in trousers, even when it became fashionable for women of a certain age to wear them. Always the classy lady.

Granny died on 14th January 1991; she was 79 years old.

A lifetime of memories from our wonderful grandparents.

Chapter 7: Music

"If music be the food of love, play on" - a famous quote from Shakespeare's great comic play, Twelfth Night.

There was love of music at Spring Farm.

If there was one thing, we all enjoyed growing up on the farm, it was music. It was in our blood. Daddy was a fabulous singer, and my brother, Derek, once said that little did Daddy know that he was sitting on a gold mine with his voice. As the saying goes, he could have made a mint.

We would have watched all the great Hollywood musicals on a Sunday afternoon, and we would sing along with the actors. Whether it be Doris Day in Calamity Jane, Bing Crosby in White Christmas, or Judy Garland in Easter Parade, we would know the words to the songs and still be singing them later that evening or for days after. I must admit, when I was young, I thought Daddy was one of the stars in the films and that he knew Frank Sinatra. His voice sounded so good and could match their talent. However, it got all of us interested in music.

We were also in the school choirs and went to the various festivals. We won so many times at the Portadown Festival and had a lovely few days at the Llangollen International Music Festival in Wales.

As predicted, we were in the church choir, and we had to sit at the front of the church. When it was time to sing our song, we would file out onto the aisle and stand in rows, with the tallest at the back. I remember having to sing the first verse of Once in Royal David's City at the Christmas carol service — I really cannot remember much about it, as I was so nervous. Although I received plenty of plaudits after the service was over. It was my one and only time singing solo in a public place!

The record player was never off, and my sisters and I danced to all the rock and roll music and tried to jive and shake ourselves to all the '60s hits. There is a lovely old wooden floor in one of the living rooms, and it was great for dancing on, especially in our socks. It was easy to move on the lovely, polished floor. We would arrange the sofa and chairs back out of the way and turn up the volume. We pulled Mummy's clothes out of her wardrobe, and we would dress up to suit the music. The sofa and chairs in that room were truly tested as we danced on them too. We would dance in front of visitors, and when Cat Stevens was number one with 'Matthew and Son,' I took the lead to show everyone how to dance to the words and music. I am sure the visitors thought I was a right show-off.

Then, of course, came the seventies, and my older sisters enjoyed T-Rex, Slade, Roxy Music, and many more great groups of that era. We loved all the colourful clothes of that decade, and it was fun wearing bell-bottom trousers. The late seventies and the great disco era were more my style of music. Barry White was my favourite, along with Stevie Wonder and Diana Ross. Also, during that time, we had the fabulous films of Grease and Saturday Night Fever — timeless music. John Travolta was a fantastic dancer, and of course, we all tried to copy his moves. I do not think we will ever recover from trying to re-enact his moves! He must have had no bones.

As I have written earlier in my book, I enjoyed my piano lessons with Mrs Hayes. I loved her piano and how she taught her pupils. Practising the scales for the piano exams was difficult, but I passed them and then got my certificates to prove it. I especially loved playing Christmas carols, and it made Christmas for me come alive at the farm. The Christmas songs on the radio always caught my attention, and I used to try to play the tune on the piano – unfortunately, nine times out of ten, it sounded nothing like the real thing on the radio. It is funny what catches a child's attention and makes what they are doing more attention-grabbing for them.

My sister, Amanda, also went to Mrs Hayes for piano lessons. She was a good pianist, too.

The room in which the piano was at the farm was at the front of the house, and it was a very stunning room. Full of antiques and beautiful furniture. The piano itself, and it is still there, has a magical design and is old-fashioned with candle holders at each side. I did put candles in them once and tried to play under their light. To my horror, the keys got covered in candle wax, and it took a while to get the piano cleaned before my parents saw it.

Daddy would have played a few notes on the piano too when he was learning a new song for singing solo in church or at a concert. He also played the accordion in Kildarton Accordion Band. He did try to get us to join the band, but that was without success — we had no interest. We had other ideas, like climbing the apple trees in the farm's orchard or jumping across the stream to the small houses we had built to play in!

The radio was never off in the kitchen, and it was tuned to so many stations. Radio One, Radio Two, and Radio Ulster for the news. I remember when I was young and my future brother-in-law, Brian, would tune the radio to Radio Caroline in the evening. Of course, the radio then was called the wireless. I will have to admit I still call it the wireless from time to time, and people do laugh at the remark. I cannot help it, as that is what I referred to it as when I was growing up.

Songs on the radio that would be playing when we were young were records made by Helen Shapiro, Cliff Richard, the Everly Brothers, and so many more. Those songs were timeless, and we still sing them — classic tunes.

I had a Great-Uncle Eric Ewart who was so musical that he played the organ and sang at concerts throughout the country. He played with Big Tom and the Mainliners and for Gloria Hunniford when she was starting out on her career. He was a comedian too, and the various concert halls around the country were packed with people when they heard he would be on the list of entertainers. When we arrived at the venue, and if he were on stage and he saw us, he would make sure that we were the centre of attention.

Mummy and Daddy tried to teach us to dance the waltz as they thought the way we danced to the music was just like we were shaking ourselves, and would say to us, "That's not dancing." I know that we stood on their toes many times when they were trying their hardest to teach us. The waltz is a gracious dance, and you just glide around the floor.

In the car, when Mummy and Daddy were taking us somewhere, we would put the car radio on. We would be singing away in the back of the car and hanging out the car windows, swaying to the sound of the music. Our parents were always telling us to behave, or they would turn the radio off. Of course, the volume had to be turned up — dear help our parents trying to have a conversation while we sang and jumped about in the back of the car. No seatbelts at that time, and just our wild, free spirit.

Even when we were on our swings, my sisters and I would be singing songs like, My Bonnie (lies over the ocean) and the Tennessee Wig Walk — an absolute favourite. Sometimes we would sing out of tune for a laugh, and it would sound so comical.

Because Daddy was such a fantastic singer, people would tease us to sing. For years, we could and can still sing, but Daddy's voice was special and in a league of its own. It was due to his singing, and Mummy's love of music too, that we loved and still love music so much. You could even hear Daddy singing in the milking parlour when he was milking the cows.

One person who always joined us if we were dancing and had great fun with us was Granny Magwood. She would do a jig and have us lying on the ground rolling about laughing. Or she would try and copy our moves and shake herself too. She was quite a mischief.

There is nothing like a singsong and the happiness it brings. It certainly brought happiness to our home.

Chapter 8: Imaginary Friends

Well, here we go. My imaginary friends kept me entertained for hours on end. I had fifteen in total, and I still cannot believe it. They kept me occupied, and I just let my imagination run wild with them.

Their names were Seana Keana, her husband, John Keana, and their baby, Baby Keana. Then there was Jarton and May May. I really do not know how I came up with their names, but there you have it.

I had hours of fun with my imaginary friends, and my family still talks about them today.

Seana Keana always reminded me of Dusty Springfield, with her beehive hair, sixties dresses and coats, cigarettes, and broad accent. Her husband, John, was a handsome, dark-haired man. Dressed well and would stay at home with Baby Keana. Gosh, I must have been ahead of my time in thinking of the woman going out to work and the man at home. John Keana was quiet and kept himself to himself.

Jarton was a bit like Ena Sharples out of Coronation Street and would be the biggest gossip. While May May always reminded me of Lulu, the singer and actor. Bubbly and funny, nice, friendly face, and wore nice, freshly ironed dresses every day.

They all lived in pretend houses in the backyard at the farm, and I would call for them in the morning and take them to work. Seana Keana worked in a pretend shop halfway up the avenue, and Jarton and May May worked in the pretend bank close to the shop where Seana was employed. I cycled to the end of the avenue to where the pretend airport was, as I was, of course, an air hostess in this great, imaginative world of mine.

When it was time to go home, I would pick them all up at their workplaces, and we would talk and chat on our way home. As usual, Jarton was gossiping about all the customers that had come to the bank that day, and May May would be telling her to be quiet. Seana would just roll her eyes as if to say, "Here we go again." Another journey with Jarton, complaining about everything under the sun.

When I got a bit bored of my five imaginary friends, I made up more, and they became: Good Seana Keana, Good John Keana, Good Baby Keana, Good Jarton, and Good May May. All the good imaginary friends were all nice, sweet, and wholesome. Even Jarton was always on her best behaviour as the gossip, but in a more constructive way.

All the so-called 'Good' imaginary friends also lived in pretend houses in the farmyard – the sheds were full. They, too, worked in the same places as their namesakes, and I gave them lifts on my bike to and from work, and if they needed to go anywhere.

Believe it or believe it not – when I became bored with all of them, I made up more imaginary friends. This time it was Bad Seana Keana, Bad John Keana, Bad Baby Keana, Bad Jarton, and Bad May May. Bringing it all to a total of fifteen!

This is where things started to get serious, as things boiled over with all the different personalities, and there was war once or twice. And I had to do a couple of runs to get them all to work on time. It was total mayhem. Either way, they gave me tremendous fun during my childhood.

My siblings still tease me about my imaginary friends, as there were so many of them, and they often ask me where I got the names from - I can only reply it was my great imagination that helped me!

Chapter 9: Trips to the Big Smoke

Oh, how we loved going to Belfast for shopping trips once or twice a year. The excitement was palpable the day before, as we would be discussing the shops we would visit and what we wanted to buy.

The day started early for us, as we had to catch the train at Portadown railway station. Daddy would have someone cover for him at the farm for the day, as we would not be home until late in the evening, and I am sure he did not want to start milking cows after a day walking around Belfast.

Our parents packed us into the car, and off we went on our day's adventure to the city. We chatted in the car about our trip, and we had our parents demented in the car, asking them so many questions. Always the same questions: what time we will arrive in Belfast, will it be raining, will there be a lot of people, and so it went on.

The journey on the train did not seem to take too long, and once we saw the nurses' homes, the tall towers at the end of the motorway, we knew we were there. We even started to put our coats on before the train had come to a halt.

Mummy and Daddy would hold on tight to us, especially the younger ones, and make the older ones walk in front so they could keep an eye on us. The pushing and shoving of people started almost immediately as we got off the train. I do not think we ever got used to that, as growing up in the country was quiet and calm.

To get to the main shops, we had to go through barriers where the security guards checked us. This was all to do with the terrorist activity that was raging around us in those years and, unfortunately, for years to come. Mummy's handbag was opened and searched not only at the barriers but also when we went into any shop. This became such a habit that when I first visited London in 1986, when I walked into a shop, I went over to the security guard at the main door and opened my handbag, only for the security guard to give me a curious look, and I had to apologise and explain my reason for doing so!

Our favourite shops were Anderson & McAuley, C&A, Robinson & Cleaver, as it housed Miss Selfridge, and of course, Marks & Spencer. They all seemed to us to be enormous in comparison to the shops at home in Armagh. Although, we did have the fantastic department stores of Lennox and Walkers in Armagh. Now, both are sadly gone.

It must have been difficult for our parents to keep a watch over us in the bustling streets and shops in Belfast. Lunch was a welcome break for us, as we were quite tired after our early start and carrying our shopping bags. In the restaurant, we marvelled at the noise, the hustle and bustle of people coming and going, the décor, and the wonderful food we got to eat. Mummy and Daddy would explain to us where we were, would mention the city landmarks that would be close by, and that we would visit them after having a bite to eat.

Soon, our day in Belfast would end, and we would make our way back to the train station for the journey home. We were always quieter homeward bound, as the excitement and walking around the streets would have made us tired. We would just play with toys on the train, and most of us were half asleep in the car from Portadown to Armagh. Bedtime was welcomed, and as soon as our heads hit the pillows, we were fast asleep.

Another day out in Belfast was the annual Balmoral Show, which is held by the Royal Ulster Agricultural Society. It goes on for over three days, and people come from all parts of the country to see it. The people are mostly from farming backgrounds, but the show does attract people who are curious to see all that is happening in the farming world.

Again, it was another early start for me and my family. Car to Portadown and then train to Belfast again. Mummy would have us dressed in our finery. I really do not know where she got the time and energy for it all. She would be dressed, too, with her Lady Member badge on, and Daddy would be dressed in a suit with his Member badge on show. We were proud of those badges as they looked especially important.

The show is held during the month of May, so it is pleasant weather enjoyed by everyone looking around the sheds full of animals and stalls selling farming products. And, of course, the food stalls, always a queue at those. Not one of us minded queuing for fish fingers, chips, and a fizzy drink. It would keep us quiet for at least twenty minutes and give our parents a break.

I loved to see the large bulls being paraded by a man in a white coat. They were enormous and seemed to get bigger every year. Even our father used to revere their size. They must have eaten their owners out of house and home, as the saying goes! The bulls were so clean and walked proudly around the arena. Everyone in their midst stopped to admire them as they passed by.

Mummy and Daddy having their badges meant that we could also enter areas where non-badge-wearing people could not. One such area was the Milk Marketing Board caravan, where we would sit down and have the free food and drinks available. Daddy would, of course, start talking to other farmers around him, while Mummy had to try and control my siblings and me from eating all the biscuits on the tables.

We would listen to the elderly farmers reminiscing about how they would have farmed the land and how they tried to understand all the new machinery and new ways of working in the farming community. It was interesting hearing it all, even though we were quite young at the time.

We spent the remainder of the day exploring the King's Hall, where there would be stalls of all sorts of items for sale, more animals, people, and, of course, the obligatory eateries.

From time to time, we would get cross with each other as we got tired walking around the show, and Mummy and Daddy had to try and take our minds off it by pointing out something out of the ordinary. I loved the book stalls and would rummage through all the shelves for a book for my parents to buy for me. I also quite liked the organ stall, as I adored music, and there was usually someone playing one of the organs, and people would stand and admire the talented organist and clap when the playing was over.

One final jaunt before we left the show for another year was to watch the show jumping taking place in the main arena late in the afternoon. We would hold our heads in our hands if the horse or pony knocked over a jump or fell. It was much worse if the rider had come off and took a while to get to their feet; a bit traumatic for children to see. The riders would be dressed in their riding attire, and at the end, the winning rider and horse were awarded a lovely rosette for their efforts.

We would head home chatting about what we had seen at the show, and the next day at school, we would tell our school chums all about it, and some of us would write about it in our homework. The children and the teacher loved to hear about our day at the Balmoral Show, even though it was the same story every year. But it was still exciting for primary school children.

Photographs

Spring Farm during the 1990s

Granny Davidson with Brenda and Lesley at the front of the farm

Great-Granny Ewart, Lesley, Brenda, Sandra, and Granny Magwood at Cranfield

Derek playing with his toys on Christmas Day

Me, Lesley, and Granda Magwood
going for a swim at Cranfield.

Mummy, Daddy with Brenda and Lesley

Granda Magwood, and his football team – he is holding the ball!

Mummy and Granny Magwood having a break!

Lesley, Sandra, and Brenda playing in the backyard.

My Great-Granda Ewart with his sons sitting on the Mall wall.

Amanda playing in the sand at Cranfield.

A painting of Spring Farm during the 1970s by Great-Uncle Hampton Ewart

Attending a wedding in Warrenpoint.

Daddy in the Armagh Royal School Rugby Team - back row 3rd from right

Daddy's family at Spring Farm

Granda Magwood outside one of the Victorian greenhouses in the garden at Spring Farm

Granny and Granda Davidson's
wedding photo.

Granny Magwood, Great-Auntie Gaynor, Great-Granny Ewart and Mummy relaxing on the Mall in Armagh

Melanie and Gail

Mummy and Daddy at church.

Mummy and her brother, Wendell

Mummy with her dog Juno

Mummy with her parents and brother, Wendell

Great-Great-Uncle John (Jap) Walker
played for Ireland and is a maternal
great-uncle to Mike Gibson

Great-Great-Uncle Joseph Cole - killed on the first day of the Battle of the Somme

Granny Magwood is being mischievous as usual!

Getting ready for a party in the large garden at the farm - Summer 2023

My grandfather's milk bottles -
Spring Farm Dairy

The beautiful piano at Spring Farm

Spring Farm during the 1980s